Love Spell

Lluvonia Graham

Presentation by *BookLeaf Publishing*

Web: www.bookleafpub.com

E-mail: info@bookleafpub.com

ISBN: 9789358312218

First edition 2023

Mother...your words have always held a magical power over me and inspired me to express my own emotions through writing. Now, as I lay my pen to paper, I am reminded of the beautiful tapestry you wove and it makes me hope that my own words, fueled by the fires that burn within me, will envelop and inspire those who walk with me on this journey, just as your words have always led and guided me.

ACKNOWLEDGEMENT

Some have come in like a summer wind…warm, comforting and brief.

Some come like hurricanes…fitful, soaking and disruptive.

Others were like fire…purifying in their destruction, beautiful in their ferocity.

The best of you are constant…consistent in your concentric path that leads your life to mine…I have been blessed by the intersection.

But you are all here within these pages and I have been forever blessed that you have been part of my journey.

"Confidence"

Confidence...

Pure confidence.

That's what attracted me to you.

The swagger of your walk...the intensity of your stare...that smile that brightens up the room.

All confidence.

When I speak to you, I find myself bound by words.

Mere nouns and adjectives do not possess the grammatical capabilities to express all the indecencies...

that I want to do

- to you.

Fingers entwined in the ideas flowing from my mind, caresses so deep that

metaphor causes simile to grind against the figure of my speech.

All the while creating eruptions of phenomes and pheromones.

Synonyms and antonyms cannot suppress the distress that churning...

burning...

deep in my soul.

Disturbing my peace...

bringing me release.

Grinding...grinding...grinding into my assonance

thrusting into my consonance

devastating my resistance.

Hold me close, as the juices of my verbal assault
saturate your intellectual crevices.

"The Birth of Poetry"

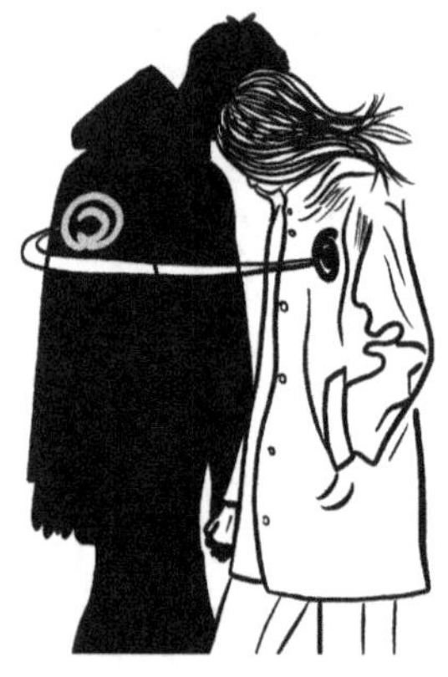

There was one, fighting alone, giving a home of solace to those who had no place to go. A shining light…a beacon…for all to see sometimes beaten, sometimes bruised, but always a glimmer...She was called Hope.

Then there was another, He being strong living in the minds of millions, sometimes suffering trying to find a way out, fighting for truth freedom and justice. Oftentimes his mission blocked by his cousin Conformity, he continued to fight, to move the one that would seduce the many. His name--Inspiration.

One day Hope and Inspiration met in a land called Turmoil and each began to wonder how they ever lived without the other. Hope expressed how hard it was to fight against the Dark. She said it tried to devour her at every turn, would dash her with waters of faithlessness and now her home, that once lay in the hearts of man...no longer existed.

Inspiration felt her pain and through her pain he found strength, courage and a way to break free of Conformity. He told her that he needed her that he no longer wanted to fight alone, he said their only hope, and his only need was to bond with her...to become one with her. On that night, they came together in a clash of emotion and thought. Her persistence enveloped his intellect, both fed their need, and on that night Hope became impregnated by Inspiration and Purpose grew in her womb.

As a child, Purpose was often misunderstood. Called horrible names like "Ambition" and "Misdirected-ness", but because Purpose was born with the genetic embellishment of resilience, she continued on- using every trial, every tribulation, every breath as fodder for her intellectual capacities.

As time passed and Purpose grew, she understood that the words that flowed through her veins weren't for her at all, didn't even belong to her. As she matured she saw ideas blossom, die and be reborn - just as she did. She saw her mother's home that lay in the hearts of men begin to swell with the remnants of her father and she longed for a way to set them free. She paced. She turned this way and that. She heard the song of Joy and the laughter of Truth. She heard the thoughts of Righteousness and felt the warmth of Love.

Try as she might she couldn't find a way to set these emotions, these new beings inside her free. She decided that she no longer wanted the responsibility of being the pulse of nations, the heartbeat of the underdog, the savior of a people. So she escaped. She left her land of peace and beauty and went to the only place she knew she wouldn't have to feel, or think or even be.

She went to the land of... Ignorance.

She drowned her sorrows in a pint of Monosyllabic Small Talk, and chased them down with a shot of Shattered Dreams.

Then, as she was walking in the land of
Ignorance, holding her purse tightly, running to
her car, locking her door, starting it as quickly as
she could, she remembered the words her
mother told her.

"No matter how blissful Ignorance seems to be,
that is not the place for you. You cannot dwell
there. You were created to lead others through
the darkness."

And at that moment with Conformity breathing
down her neck, chasing her into a dark alley,
when she felt the world begin to collapse into
doldrums and mediocrity. Conformity, she
picked up a pen and she began to write.

She wrote about Love and Hate, politics and
civilities, men and women, darkness and light-
Truth and Justice. She wrote about the past, the
future, the ins and outs and the ups and downs of
the human experience.

The concrete was watered with her tears and if
they could be counted, it would be like counting
the drops of rain.

And at that moment...she became more than
Purpose...she became Poetry.

"I Hear Bells"

When I think of you- I hear bells. Not bells that alarm with the harshness of sound, but bells that alert me to new opportunities, new reasons for living. New chances to see you.

While watering the buds of intellectual thought that germinate in rows before me, I am reminded of the flowering emotions I feel with the sounding of the bell. Each passing shadow outside my door, each rising and setting of the sun, signals a conflicting feeling--anticipation at the sight of you- ache at the absence of you.

My eyes gaze steadily at the objects of my stewardship but my inner eye constantly awaits your arrival in its peripheral. A constant dance inside the ring where delusion jabs reality and primal urges sucker punch civility in the jaw.

The bell rings again and this time with the entering and exiting of hopeful futures, I am perplexed at the sadness I feel due to lost opportunities...of a lost presence...of a Paradise Lost armed with the archaic derisive devices of etiquette, ethics, and political correctness, that in their fury cause us to leap into martyrdom and massacre the need to...the joy felt by...the drive to cohabitate that lies deeply seeded within us both.

The bell rings again and this time I am waiting for the moment- the instant- I sense movement. Heart beating fast, palms sweating, face illuminated- I sense you. You are here.

Sensing the concealed warmth from me you are guided to me- a missile to its target. Seeking heat from you, I allow you access to my airspace with clear passage and smooth intentions. You enter armed with a lethal smile and loaded guns. I- quivering with adrenaline- determine fight or flight choosing to ascend on heralded wings to the safe airspace of cloud nine.

War is waged and peace is forged in one fleeting moment...while the world watches.

With a glance, we both decide to live and fight another day...

And then the bell rings.

"How Do You Love a Black Man?'

How do you love a Black Man when he can't love himself?

You must first teach him what it means to be loved. This is truly what he knows, but he has forgotten because Mama's love does not extend to the boardroom, the courtroom or even the classroom. You must teach him his value, his worth, his strength. Teach him that his visage was made in the image of the most high, that his voice is meant to command a sea of thousands, that his loins will father generations...teach him...because the world will whip it out of him.

How do you love a Black Man when he can't
love himself?

You show him, because what he sees on the TV-
the world believes. You show him that he is not
the carjacking, thieving, robbing, lying,
cheating, wife-beating, dream-stealing,
heartbreaking, pimping, hustling hatemongering
villain that the world would have the universe
believe he'd be. You show him that he is the
Father, the Sun, the Blessed One that God meant
him to be.

How do you love a Black Man when he can't
love himself?

You believe in him because everyday is filled
with doubt; he walks in this man's land and he
sees throughout. He searches high and low for
acceptance, trust and admiration but finds only
hate, mistrust and isolation. He is searching,
seeking, hoping to find a place of rest to soothe
his troubled mind.

How do you love a Black Man when the world
dares him to love himself?

You love you because you are him. Creamy
shades of cocoa and brown, of deepest blue and

royal black. You love you because it is you he lacks. You are his helpmate, his soul mate, his queen- you are the moon for which his sun beams. Your love of him is a reflection of you, continuously connected, each being one of the two- inexplicably intertwined with a destiny yet to be fulfilled, your need of him equals his love of you, two loves brandishing one power with one home to build.

Love him strong, love him deep. Love high enough that when he cries you weep because he is your son, your husband, your father, your brother, your love, your life, your protector, your lover. When the day is rough give a non-judgmental shoulder, rub him with ointments when his body has grown older.

I ask you again, my daughter...my sister...my mother...

How do you love a Black Man when the world dares him to love himself?

You love him...you love him...you love him because you were created for him...he and no other else.

"The Night"

The night was cool and wet. It had been so
hot earlier in the day the people of the town had
resorted to laying in bed naked praying for the
rain to come, praying for God to wash the night
sky with the tears of a people tired of running in
the same circle, living the same impossible
dream. On this night the only activity came from
the constant buzzing of insects, and the air was
so silent that you could hear the blessed rain
falling in teardrops from the leaves of the trees.

The humidity clung to me like a second skin.
I could feel it wrapping me in a blanket of
warmth and security. The moisture invigorated
me, rejuvenated me and inspired me. I felt
invincible. I was invincible. It was the kind of
weather in which you could be uninhibited and
free while the universe watched.

The sight of His car ripped me from my
thoughts. I watched him as a cat watches its prey
before it pounces and waited for Him to realize
that I wasn't there. I could tell by the way His
car stopped at the end of the drive that he was
surprised I wasn't there yet. Any other time I
was so anxious to see Him, to be part of Him, to

be one with Him that I would arrive early and wait to see him approach me.

His approach was that of a King. There was none like it. He was always so self-assured, so decisive that I couldn't help but watch him. He didn't just walk; He commanded the earth and stars to move at his leisure. He was a lion, commanding all the earth as His jungle...and I was His prey...but tonight the hunter has become the hunted.

I pulled my car into the drive behind his, waited, then circled around to face him. I could see, even through the tinted windows, the smile that crossed his face. The smile that signified His award had arrived. His comfort, his strength, his sanctuary from the ordinary and per functionary. The smile that says I am his and he has claimed me. Through the mist on my window, I watch him as he takes his time leaving the car. He watches me just as closely as I watch him and I become aware of a flush in my cheeks, a heart that skips a beat, and a smile that lights the night.

As he enters my car the scent of him overtakes me and instantly I am knocked into a sensual spasm. His scent is that of wisdom, of courage, of outrage, of strength, of struggle, of blessing and of raw maleness. I am entranced and beguiled; I am his prisoner. Fighting to free

myself from a gaze so consuming I feel weak
under the weight of it. I begin to make casual
conversation.

"How are you?"
   "Good."
"Did you miss me?"
   "Did you miss me?"
"Tell me."
   "No."
"Because I want you to?"
   "Ugh hugh."

The subject changes to many different
subjects, none of them what we want to speak
about. We spend many minutes trying to be
civilized, trying to act like adults, still collapsing
into giggles when we try. Looking at each other
in silence, reading each other's thoughts,
wondering what the other is thinking, knowing
anyway.
   Then the night takes over and I am not my
own. My hand finds his stomach and feels the
ridges of him; he sighs and moves my hand
away. I come to him again and this time I lift his
shirt to see my prize and run my nails along his
chest, he groans and pushes me away. This is not
his way, not how he sees it, not under his
control. My motives are questioned as is his

fidelity, the questions are pointed, but playful, neither of us meaning any of it. We fight for control, who will win, who will conquer? I sit with ego slightly reddened as he looks at me with those eyes. Pools of longing and conflict and lust. He tells me that he wants me and I tell him that I am his.

We leave our public meeting place to find our private corner along one of the back roads. I drive practically on autopilot for we have been here before, but never at night, and definitely not on this night, this night when the only activity came from the constant buzzing of insects, and the air was so silent that you could hear the blessed rain falling in teardrops from the leaves of the trees.

I stop the car and the temperature rises to intolerable degrees. He takes my hand to lead the way and before I move I take his fingers into my mouth to let him know that each of them is a mirror of what will later come.

I tell him to get in the back seat and he seems anxious, I know not why, he obeys, and I bend my knees in worship to the temple of his body. He, ever the gracious teacher, guides me and encourages me to love him moaning softly, eyes closed. His anxiousness gets the best of him and he breathes softly into the night air, "I want that pussy." Shivers run all over me and I am so very happy to oblige. Opening the car door I enter the night air, the air in which you could be uninhibited and free while the universe watched. I feel dizzy and drunk with the need for him and I position myself on the hood of the car so that he can enter me from behind and he pulled back and told me that he wanted me "with my legs in the air." I knew what that meant, he wanted complete control of me, he wanted me vulnerable and under his complete control and I was happy to give myself to him. He laid me in the backseat and I opened my love for him. He entered me like a man who knows where he belongs, a man who is confident and free. There in front of God and everyone- I was his and he was mine.

We spent many minutes trying to be civilized, trying to act like adults, still collapsing into giggles when we tried. Looking at each other in silence, reading each other's thoughts, wondering what the other is thinking- knowing anyway.

"Ode to a Young Widow"

You gave him all you had to give: your youth,
your beauty, your will to live.
At night you wait patiently for him to come
home only to know that you are to spend this
night alone.
Crying, ranting, raving, listening for the phone,
no matter what you do, still alone.
Begging, pleading, given no reprieve you start to
hate him so much you wish he would leave.

Lying to your friends and family telling them
that the marriage ended happily- hoping that
your virtue will be rewarded aptly.

Putting on your very best smile… knowing that
he lies all the while… hoping that it will be over
soon so that you can sleep…just go ahead and
bury the Creep!

Assassination

To kill a man, you must first assassinate his
character.
The character of the black man is sitting in the
balcony and the assassins won't wait. We have
been wedded to calamity and the guests are
throwing hate.
Hell has frozen over and we have not yet learned
to skate and while we try to get it together, the
world tears us apart with hate.
For you see the time for what could have been
has passed. It is our turn now, our turn at last.
This is a time for growth, determination. Focus.
Let us all rise up and cover the earth like locusts.
Be with me, follow me, let us give birth together

'cuz I've been pregnant with purpose for far too
long and babies don't stay babies forever.
I have been promised to, sworn to, and prayed
for. I will not walk sheepishly behind 40 acres
anymore. My dowry is set, in it millions or
more; the world is not yet ready for what I have
in store.
My mother raised me to remember who I am for
and now that I understand the world is my
willing paramour—sitting and waiting for me by
night, shaming the daylight with the force of my
might.

I'll come in the daytime. I don't have to sneak at
night.

There were so many before me, so many who
have tried—step aside now Mama, you will sit at
the front of this ride. I have been bred from a
world of utter contempt and damnation but I be
damn if I give in to governmental solicitation.
They poison us, repair us only to poison us
again. Hell it's simply a replay of the Tuskegee
Airmen.
If you let them tell it they are giving us a hand
out- hell from where I'm looking-- with my
credit- I don't know what that shit is about.
This is the era of taking my turn. No more New
Deals- let that shit burn. I am hopelessly,

wholeheartedly intrinsically focused. Let me
inspire you with the words of my opus.
No longer bought bamboozled or paid for…I
live in the light- not to be blinded anymore.

My Epitaph

May 23…is the day that I died.

There was no breaking news story, no interruption of the basketball game, no vigil set in my memory.
There were no cries of righteous indignation, or moral outrage…
Just emptiness and silence.
My death was not an easy one. I struggled and strained everyday fighting the disease that consumed my body, my heart, my thoughts. I cried salty tears all through the night that when I awoke the next morning, a salty trail on my

cheek was all I could remember of the painful dream that invaded my slumber.

Every morning we started our day with a, "Hey Babe." Our own special language, a language of two who were in pain…siblings in the same disease. I would go about my day with intermittent shots of light, the medicine of Joy, only every night to be racked with the pain of longing and separation.

When I went into remission, I was able to function better, work through some of the pain…to go on living, despite the knowledge of the succubus that lay in wait to release pestilence, pain and emotional famine.

I often sought the help of other, less experienced, doctors hoping that perhaps there was a cure somewhere in their eyes…latent…lying in wait for me…the perfect specimen to receive the vaccine.

But it was to no avail.

I tried more unconventional methods for a cure. I desperately tried to hypnotize myself, hoping to change my behavior, to make my immunity stronger so that I had a chance to live. But my feeble mind and organs had been so damaged that it was obviously no hope left for me.

So I did what I had to do, I pushed on. I played through the pain. I made myself believe that I was ok- that you were ok- I would, you would, be ok—without us. I lied to myself and I lied to others because the thought of living with the disease was too much for me to bear.

So here it is…here we are…the day of my death, the end of my life, the waking from my dream. Today, I will die.

I'll sit with hundreds of other people all infected at one time, but only I suffering now. I will sit, and I will laugh and I will cry and I will push through the pain.

I'll hear you say, "I do." And in that moment all joy, all peace, all love will leave this body and I will descend into the depths to be lost forever and burn with unrequited desire for that which has infected me.

My soul will depart this earth in a whisper completely dissevered from yours for as "long as you both shall live."

Ashes to ashes…dust to dust…congratulations.

May I rest…in peace.

While You Were Sleeping

While you were sleeping, I heard the angels call your name. Their voices rang in one resounding trumpet that rang from the hilltops, and thundered in the valleys-waking me so that I could watch the spectacle of a lifetime…totally stricken speechless- in awe of the sleeping masterpiece lying next to me.

While you were sleeping. I watched the winged seraphs of heaven come down and adorn your head, shoulders and torso with the light that makes women dream of romance, happily ever after, and life after death.

While you were sleeping, I thought myself an inventor who could create a bottle or some container that could hold your essence and while capturing that which is the heart of you still preserve the freedom and independence that defines you so beautifully.

I wanted so desperately to possess you but at the same time to share you with the world, your light, your intelligence- you the definition of man- the word love personified.
I wanted to shout your name from atop the highest building known to humankind in all corners of the earth to let everyone know that I have found what our grandmothers spoke about, what our mothers dreamed about, what we have hoped for…he is here…lying next to me…in all his righteous glory.

My Dark Knight. Filled with nobility, shaped and refined by the harsh environment, chiseled from the crust of the earth, clarified and deemed infracturable due to the pressure of the world that has refused to make room for him, the world he so diligently lifts to his shoulders, not just for

himself, for those he loves, those he will love
and those afraid to love.

While you were sleeping, I dreamt of you…I
dreamed of a future made clear, a night made
safe from harm, a heart able to be free.
I dreamed of renewed hopes and pleasures
untold and a soul with which my soul could
grow old.
Dear One, I dreamt of you and upon your
waking I will dream again and again and again.

A Headless Queen

A Headless queen surrounded by courtesans who believe themselves to be Cinderella perpetrating to be Snow White traveling in the Enchanted Forest. Clouded minds that leave bread crumbs to lead them back to their forgotten sensibilities.

A Headless Queen surrounded by dickless horsemen, unchivalrous creatures that seek to devour my independence by siphoning my strength and putting chains on my psyche in their best effort to cling to my aura.

There comes a time in a Queen's life when she understands, no, she has to come to terms with-some things about herself.

These realizations come in many forms. Sometimes they are small shuddering shadows of thought that stealthily creep into your existence patiently waiting for the dawn of illumination.

Other times, they are wild animals that pounce on you, ripping away the sensitive skin of your very existence leaving scars of acceptance that become permanent reminders of the price of delusion.

Better still, they are murderers that wait in the
dark alleys of your soul of pomp and
circumstance and duplicity to carjack you of
your dreams, rape you of your self-imposed
reality and leave you in the street naked for all to
see trying desperately to put Band-Aids over
bullet holes and piece together your fractured
psyche.
Better still…they may be jubilant revelations
emulating lights, emitting praise and prayers and
thankfulness while the choir provides the
musical accompaniment to your rebirth.
However the Renaissance may begin, the
Golden Age of Enlightenment will come…and it
will come with a vengeance.

You Are Mine

Simply stated: you are mine.
From the top of your head to the bottom of your
feet, from the air that you breathe to the food
that you eat…

You. Are. Mine.

I love the way my lips kiss me. Firm, confident
and warm. Sweet like honey, hot like fire and
endless in their grasp of my tongue.

I long for the way my hands touch me. Stroking me slowly, caressing me lightly, squeezing me firmly- bringing me to the apex of pleasure.

I love to watch me walk to myself…confident, assured and strong. The walk of a lion in his jungle, in his element, in his kingdom.

I wait for the moments that my eyes see me. Looking closely, deeply, longingly at me. Eyes brown like the finest chocolate, glistening like the sun on the sea.

Come…put your arms around me so that we may melt together and then into me.

Meditation on Love 1

32

The paradoxical nature of love is one that baffles its participants beyond all understanding. One that elates the spirit and pierces the soul with a mere sleight of hand.

Those of us who allow ourselves to entertain the decadent delusion care not for the punctures and punishments it lavishly languishes upon us, but live for the seldom seen semblances of trickery that only the infatuation and obsession of being in love may provide.

The enchanting embrace or soul-consuming kiss or shared seductive secret of a lover serves as promise that where one comes many more will follow- or therein lies the hope.

Retail Therapy

I saw you yesterday.
I was walking through the mall ignoring sideways glances from paired men, and the occasional catcall from those single, every moment thinking what it was this market of flesh and goods had to offer, every second wondering what consumable item would offer the "goods" to spur my budding monetary ejaculation and resulting respite and then… I saw you.
You were walking with the grace and circumstance of a dignitary, the palatable strength and pride of an athlete and the fierceness of a lion.
My body reacted, ready to pounce, to join, to connect.
I watched you walk slowly, carefully, methodically. I watched you peruse the man-made manufactured material goods and smiled as you found them not to be of your liking.
I watched as you sifted the wheat of the women in your presence and deemed them all chaff. I grinned as I watched them all blow away like grains of sand. Then, sensing me, you looked in

my direction and I was immediately drawn down
deep- and even further still- into those
cappuccino lightning infused cauldrons and you
teleported me to you.
The strength of your thoughts matched the
strength of your physical being and I stood in
front of you as our paths intersected for the
briefest of moments. You looked at me and me
at you and the resonance of recognition became
a shroud that covered us, warmed us, protected
us.
In that moment, I knew you like no other was
able to know you, felt you like no other had.
And you, you felt me, allowed your presence to
enter me, touched every part of my soul,
gathered me cerebrally and joined, we soared to
the highest heights imaginable.
Then, as quickly as it began, it was over.
I was alone and shaken from the contact. You
seemed off balance. And we both whispered a
breathless, "Excuse me" as the perpendicular
nature of our intersection carried us in different
directions.
After a moment, I turned to watch you walk
away only to see a last glimpse of lightning as
all the chaff were parted in your wake.

Then I, no longer searching for consumable
goods or sources of monetary pleasure, trembled
slightly- and returned home.

The Last Supper

Allow me to sip from your lips the warm sweet
nectar of intellect. Your words, like the softest
rain, bathe the inside of my ears washing them
so sweetly with a flood of knowledge to counter
my own, challenge my own, match my own.
Our delectable nuggets of conversation still feed
my starving brain emaciated from the lack of
nourishment. They remain to me a most
exquisite chocolate to a dying soul.
Cut for me a tenderloin of your strength.
Strength born from adversity, forged by force
and ordained by God. Feed me so that I may,
from you, retain the nutrients of perseverance,
patience, integrity, faith and serenity. Nourish
my hungry heart with hope and joy exemplified
by your trials and your struggles. Feed me your
story that I might grow strong.
Allow me, Dear One, to bask in the aroma of
your scent of passion. Take me on an olfactory
pleasure ride that starts with the warmth of the
softest kiss goodbye, gentle caresses from strong
hands followed by tongues tasting new
territories, teeth nibbling new flesh, bodies
connecting in the deepest of ways.

Penetrate my thoughts and my body with your
pain and your struggle and I give back to you,
once twice and again, the knowledge of the
fulfillment of your dreams, the fruition of your
destiny.
As I sit here at this table crying because I am no
longer able to be physically in your presence,
unable to fill the void that now remains,
understand that there is joy and happiness for
you beneath these tear stains.
Know that, Dear One, you are blessed, loved and
treasured by so many that your beauty and
strength of character are a constant reminder for
all that come in contact with you and partake in
the deliciousness of you that there is -and will
always remain- hope.
So as I take my napkin and dry my tears of
sorrow staring through blurred vision at the chair
where you once used to sit, know it is my
fondest hope for the morrow that you will see
our time together as well spent and feel as I do
that it was heaven sent.

Questions Asked and Answered

What is it about love that makes us want it so badly that we will lie to ourselves to have it?
Why do we continually neglect ourselves to give others what they need even though we know that they do not deserve it?
Why would the Father, creator of all, instill in us a need so all-consuming, all-encompassing that we would give our youth and our heart to someone who is so clearly undeserving?
Who beside the Bain of Eden should be punished in a way that no other animal could tolerate?

Why, in all existence, is it we of God's creatures
that have to be stepped on, stepped out on, lied
on and lied to, tortured and hurt by the very
same creature that is supposed to love us?
When will we be able to understand the disease
that affects us, the cancer that sickens us, the
club that beats us…the man who is supposed to
love us?
Could it be that in all actuality the enormous
amount of love and affection she feels is really
an act of desperation to hold on to her way of
life?
Is it plausible that her overwhelming need to be
near him at all times to know how he is feeling
and where he is, in actuality, is only
symptomatic of her need to control every aspect
of her life?
Are those play fights he has with her, pushing
her, tickling her until she can't take it anymore,
only whimsical versions of the ones where she
goes to the hospital?
Could it be that she is so preoccupied with her
own transgressions that she is imagining his?

Or is he so caught up in his own dirt that he is
imagining her to be soiled?

Dance with Me

Hey, Daddy.
How you doin'?
I saw you watching me from over there. No, no,
Boo. Don't get it twisted.
I don't mind.
You definitely look like you are just..my…kind.
Yea, I love to dance. I'm digging you for real
wondering if you're able to give me something I
can feel.
Wondering if you are able to make it count
because a woman like me-
I like my conversation with the lights out.
Oh you think you can handle that?

Yea, we'll see.
Come on over here and dance with me.
Put your hands on my hips- I don't bite. Yea
that's it baby. That's what I like.
Come on don't be shy.
Move a little closer, that's right closer.
I want to be able to lay my head on your
shoulder.
Come on, Daddy let me dance for you. Let your
eyes caress my body.
Let them watch me do what I do.
Oh I can feel your nature rise, you got me
wanting what's between them thighs.
That's it, Darling, fast then slow.
Let me see how low you are willing to go.
Oh yea. I like the way you move.
Keep dancing with me baby
I like the way you groove.

I Don't Even Know Your Name

I know in my heart that I've made love to you
at least a million times
in a thousand different places
in hundreds of different ways.
I know that your hands have caressed me
your lips have tasted me
and your eyes have seen me… all of me…
in a way that I have never been seen before.
What it is in you I see- I do not know.
What it is in I fear- I can only imagine.
But there is a magnetism in you I've searched
for,
craved for
desired more than anything
and it's that desire that drives me forward and
pulls me near you in a wave of heat and flame.
My soul is eternally connected to yours in a way
that can only be described as surreal,
can only be described as indescribable
can only be described as oneness.
You can never understand how the essence of
you reaches to the heart of me making me slave
to the interconnectedness that surrounds our
auras.

I'm not the only one that sees it, that feels it, that
wants it.
The connection between you and I is inescapable
is indescribable
is immeasurable.
I don't think I can ever feel this way with
anyone else as long as I live…
Be it this life- or the next.
And I don't even know your name.

My Mind is a Whore

My Mind is a Whore
She craves pleasure from many partners and
searches out variety.
There is no one member of any one society that
is too large for her to take
Too large for to bring to ejaculation through
intellectual stimulation.
Be ye Mandingo or Gringo
She needs it
She desires it
She wants it.
She wants it as much as you want the sand
between your toes
The smell of sweet potato pie in your nose
As much as you like hot peaches on your
tongue.
She craves every gifted drop, every one.
My Mind is a Whore
She'll entwine herself in the raunchiest of
positions and follow you to the darkest of alleys
and moan as you take her to the wall.
She will taunt and tease and give you intellect
after intellect because
She is capable of multiple explosions of hot
liquid summations

Without the use of fillers
Or rubber incantations.
She can lubricate your hardened mind
As you try to take her from behind.
Sucking all the life from whatever she may
find…without missing a beat.
She is the only one of her kind.
My mind is a whore…
Do you want to fuck my mind?

Who Am I?

Who am I?
I'm that girl Mama warned you about
Make ya raise ya hands, make ya holla, make ya shout.
Get down on ya knees beggin' me please,
"Baby can I please lay my head on your pillowy double D's?"
Who am I?
Oh, you ain't know?
I'm the one already out the back before you hit the front door.
Figuratively, literally intellectually equipped.
Stepping over all the puddles on which you have already slipped.
Who am I?

Still ain't got it?
Then let me tell you one more time.
The phenomic interactions I weave for you are
much too tight for you to get through and once I
get finished with you, Boo, you really won't
know what to do.
You still don't know who I am?
You better ask somebody.
Underestimate me once and you'll be sitting in
the floor
(Nose all snotty)
Wondering how I can cut you so bad and still
make you want some more.
I am somebody!
I ain't no secret agent, no Barbie doll, Nawl, I
ain't none of that shit.
I'm just that Texas girl with a fly-ass mouthpiece
that likes to
Spit
Real
Shit.

I Wish

I wish you would come to lay with me as we
wonder about the silly mechanisms of the world
and dote on our own frivolity and perspective as
we conquer them all with our words…
I wish that allowing you to touch the roundness
of me, those sensitive tender places, would allow
you to gain the complete knowledge of the fire
that burns within me and allow you to release
the tempest that reigns in you.
I wish that allowing you to feel the warmth of
my softest and most secret places, moistened
with the thought of you and heated by memories
of your touch, would embolden you to allow
yourself to take what you need…
Allow you to stretch your hands and body forth
to me and take from the deepest softest parts of

me that which gives you pleasure and will bring
you release.

Nights Like This...

It is nights like this...when the air is so still I can hear its heartbeat and the ground so cold that I feel all my warmth leave me.

It is nights like this into my mind's eye, penetrating memories of you creep.

It is nights like this...when my body aches with longing and my skin's natural glow intensifies diminishing all thought and fear of grief...

It is nights like this that memories of you come to me...and lull me into the fantasy that exists before sleep.

www.ingramcontent.com/pod-product-compliance
Lightning Source LLC
LaVergne TN
LVHW021250200726
843509LV00012B/1624